W9-AWU-841

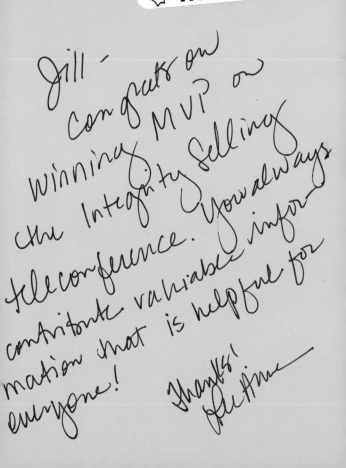

Jill -
congrats on
winning MVP on
the Integrity Selling
teleconference. You always
contribute valuable information that is helpful for
everyone!

Thanks!
[signature]

INSPIRATIONS

FOR

SUCCESS

SUSANNE STARCK

8102 Lemont Road, #300
Woodridge, IL 60517
Phone: 630-390-3580   Fax: 630-390-3585

Compiled by Susanne Starck

Cover Design by Design Dynamics
Typeset Design by Julie Otlewis

Published by Great Quotations, Inc.

Library of Congress Catalog Card Number : 98-075794

ISBN: 1-56245-367-X

Printed in Hong Kong 2004

To my friends and family for their support and encouragement.

No student ever attains very eminent success by simply doing what is required of him; it is the amount and excellence of what is over and above the required, that determines the greatness of ultimate distinction.

— Charles Kendall Adams

Success attracts success!
There is no escape from this
great universal law; therefore,
if you wish to attract success
make sure that you look the part
of success, whether your calling
is that of a day laborer or a
merchant prince.

— Napoleon Hill

You have reached the pinnacle of success as soon as you become uninterested in money, compliments, or publicity.

— O. A. Battista

Your success will always be measured by the quality and quantity of service you render.

— Earl Nightingale

Success has always been easy
to measure. It is the distance
between one's origins and
one's final achievement.

— Michael Korda

Would you like me to give you a formula for success? It's quite simple, really. Double your rate of failure ... You're thinking of failure as the enemy of success. But it isn't at all. You can be discouraged by failure - or you can learn from it. So go ahead and make mistakes. Make all you can. Because, remember that's where you'll find success. On the far side of failure.

— Thomas J. Watson

Notice the difference between what happens when a man says to himself, "I have failed three times" and what happens when he says, "I am a failure."

— S. I. Hayakawa

We do not do well except when we know where the best is and when we are assured that we have touched it and hold its power within us.

— Joseph Joubert

I can give you a six-word formula for success: Think things through - then follow through.

— Eddie Rickenbacker

Do not wait to strike till the
iron is hot; but make it hot
by striking.

— William B. Sprague

Success in life comes not from holding a good hand, but in playing a poor hand well.

— Dennis Waitley and Remi L. Witt

You must realize that failure is
one of the success forces,
and to get the opportunity to
fail is also to be able to increase
your opportunity for success in
the future.

— Joseph Sugarman

When I am delivering my
very best, then that is when
I feel successful.

— Art Fettig

To be successful: Do the things you know you should do. Don't do the things you know you should not do.

If you act successful, people will treat you as such, and you will get many opportunities to achieve.

A tragic irony of life is that we so often achieve success of financial independence after the chief reason for which we sought it has passed away.

— Ellen Glasgow

Do what most people don't do and you'll be successful.

— Jim Nussbaum

Success means only doing what you do well, letting someone else do the rest.

— Goldstein's Truism

To be successful you have to be lucky, or a little mad, or very talented, or find yourself in a rapid growth field.

— Edward De Bono

Success is simply a matter of luck.
Ask any failure.

— Earl Wilson

To have known the best, and to
have known it for the best is
success in life.

— John W. MacKay

Apparent failure may hold in
its rough shell the germs of a
success that will blossom in time,
and bear fruit throughout
the eternity.

— Frances Ellen Watkins

For the people who are diligent,
who show that they merit success,
society has great rewards.

Share your vision of success with your employees. It's something they can win if they put out the effort. They'll get excited about success when they know you're excited.

— Nicholas V. Luppa

I have learned that success is to
be measured not so much by
the position that one has reached
in life as by the obstacles which
he has overcome while trying
to succeed.

— Booker T. Washington

The first step towards success
in any occupation is to become
interested in it.

— Sir William Osler

The talent of success is nothing more than doing what you can do well; and doing well whatever you do, without a thought of fame.

— Henry Wadsworth Longfellow

Success is a trendy word.
Don't aim for success if you
want it; just do what you love
and it will come naturally.

— David Frost

There is no royal road to success.
Work is the keynote.

— George G. Williams

Try not to become a man of success but rather to become a man of value.

— Albert Einstein

Let me say to you and to myself in one breath: Cultivate the tree which you have found to bear fruit in your soil. Regard not your past failures or successes. All the past is equally a failure and a success; it is a success in as much as it offers you the present opportunity.

— Henry David Thoreau

Success is not so much
achievement as achieving.
Refuse to join the cautious crowd
that plays not to lose;
play to win.

— David J. Mahoney

The man who succeeds has a program. He first sets his course and adheres to it. He sets his plans and executes them. He goes straight to his goal.

— Orison Swett Marden

No matter what you do, do it to
your utmost. I always attribute
my success to always requiring
myself to do my level best, if
only in driving a tack in straight.

— Russell H. Conwell

Success is ninety-nine percent mental attitude. It calls for love, joy, optimism, confidence, serenity, poise, faith, courage, cheerfulness, imagination, initiative, tolerance, honesty, humility, patience and enthusiasm.

— Wilfred A. Peterson

I do not know anyone who has gotten to the top without hard work. That is the recipe. It will not always get you to the top, but it should get you pretty near.

— Margaret Thatcher

It takes less work to succeed than to fail.

— W. Clement Stone

For you to be successful, sacrifices must be made. It's better that they are made by others but failing that, you'll have to make them yourself.

— Rita Mae Brown

You can have anything you want if you want it desperately enough. You must want it with an inner exuberance that erupts through the skin and joins the energy that created the world.

— Sheila Graham

To succeed, it is necessary to accept the world as it is and rise above it.

— Michael Korda

When a man feels throbbing
within him the power to do what
he undertakes as well as it can
possibly be done, and all of his
faculties say "amen" to what he is
doing, and give their unqualified
approval to his efforts, -
this is happiness, this is success.

— Orison Swett Marden

Nobody succeeds beyond his or her wildest expectations unless he or she begins with some wild expectations.

— Ralph Charell

The seed of success is service.
Put service first and success takes
care of itself.

Your success depends on the
success of the people around you.

— Benjamin H. Bristol

Success can make you go one of two ways. It can make you a prima donna, or it can smooth the edges, take away the insecurities, let the nice things come out.

— Barbara Walters

The toughest thing about success
is that you've got to keep on
being a success.

— Irving Berlin

The man who will use his skill and constructive imagination to see how much he can give for a dollar instead of how little he can give for a dollar is bound to succeed.

— Henry Ford

Self trust is the first secret
of success.

— Emerson

Why not select the right role, the
role of a successful person -
and rehearse it?

— Maxwell Maltz

My formula for success?
Rise early, work late, strike oil.

— J. Paul Getty

The successful man will profit
from his mistakes and try again
in a different way.

— Dale Carnegie

Success is the child of drudgery
and perseverance. It can not be
coaxed or bribed; pay the price
and it is yours.

— Orison Swett Marden

If you wish success in life, make perseverance your bosom friend, experience your wise counselor, caution your elder brother and hope your guardian genius.

— Joseph Addison

Watch out for emergencies.
They are your big chance!

— Fritz Reiner

The success of any great moral
enterprise does not depend
on numbers.

— William Lloyd Garrison

The ultimate of being successful
is the luxury of giving yourself
the time to do what you want
to do.

— Leontyne Price

Every failure is a step to success.

— William Whewell

As a general rule the most
successful man in life is the man
who has the best information.

— Benjamin Disraeli

Every successful man I have heard of has done the best he could with conditions as he found them.

— Edgar W. Howe

Success is having the courage
to meet failure without
being defeated.

Talk success, think success,
act like a success, look like one.

— Orison Swett Marden

If you achieve success, you will get applause, and if you get applause, you will hear it.
My advice to you concerning applause is this: Enjoy it but never quite believe it.

— Robert Montgomery

The first step toward success is taken when you refuse to be a captive of the environment in which you first find yourself.

— Mark Caine

The greatest thing a man can do in this world is to make the most possible out of the stuff that has been given him. This is success, and there is no other.

— Orison Swett Marden

I owe my success to having listened respectfully to the very best advice, and then going away and doing the exact opposite.

— G. K. Chesterton

All you need is the plan, the road map, and the courage to press on to your destination.

— Earl Nightingale

The most important single ingredient in the formula of success is knowing how to get along with people.

— Theodore Roosevelt

It isn't by size that you win
or fail - be the best of whatever
you are.

— Douglas Malloch

Those who tell you it's tough
at the top have never been
at the bottom.

— Peter Potter

If at first you don't succeed you
are running about average.

— M. H. Alderson

Success in its highest and noblest form calls for peace of mind and enjoyment and happiness which come only to the man who has found the work that he likes best.

— Napoleon Hill

Never lose sight of the fact that the most important yardstick of your success will be how you treat other people - your family, friends, and coworkers, and even strangers you meet along the way.

— Barbara Bush

What an individual thinks or feels as success is unique with him. In our experience we have found that each individual has a different meaning of, and attitude toward, what constitutes success.

— Alfred Adler

Success is that old ABC - ability,
breaks, and courage.

— Charles Luckman

You have succeeded in life when
all you really want is only what
you really need.

— Vernon Howard

Not to the swift, the race;
Not to the strong, the fight;
Not to the righteous, perfect grace:
Not to the wise, the light.
But often faltering feet
Come surest to the goal;
And they who walk in darkness meet
The sunrise of the soul.

— Henry Van Dyke

To follow, without halt, one aim;
That's the secret of success.

— Anna Pavlova

No one has a corner on success.
It is his who pays the price.

— Orison Swett Marden

Making a success of the job at hand is the best step toward the kind you want.

— Bernard M. Baruch

I made a resolve then that I was
going to amount to something if
I could. And no hours, nor amount
of labor, nor amount of money
would deter me from giving the
best that there was in me.
And I have done that ever since,
and I win by it. I know.

— Colonel Harland Sanders

Even when people are more successful than they had imagined, nothing is ever achieved without giving something up.

— Judith M. Bardwick

Success or failure is often
determined on the
drawing board.

— Robert J. McKain

When a man has done his best, has given his all, and in the process supplied the needs of his family and his society, that man has made a habit of succeeding.

— Mack R. Douglas

Success is harnessing your heart
to a task you love to do. It is
falling in love with your work.
It demands intense concentration
on your chief aim in life. It is
focusing the full power of all you
are on what you have a burning
desire to achieve.

It is a mark of many famous people that they cannot part with their brightest hour; what worked once must always work.

— Lillian Hellman

Failures want pleasing methods
...successes want pleasing results.

— Earl Nightingale

We must do the best we can with what we have.

— Edward Rowland Sill

True success is overcoming the fear of being unsuccessful.

— Paul Sweeney

Other Titles by Great Quotations, Inc.

Great Quotations, Inc.
8102 Lemont Road, #300
Woodridge, IL 60517
Phone: 630-390-3580   Fax: 630-390-3585

Other Titles by Great Quotations, Inc.

Paperbacks

I'm Not Over the Hill
Life's Lessons
Looking for Mr. Right
Midwest Wisdom
Mommy & Me
Mother, I Love You
The Mother Load
Motivating Quotes
Mrs.Murphy's Laws
Mrs. Webster's Dictionary
Only A Sister
The Other Species
Parenting 101
Pink Power
Romantic Rhapsody
The Secret Langauge of Men
The Secret Langauge of Women
The Secrets in Your Name
A Servant's Heart
Social Disgraces
Stress or Sanity
A Teacher is Better Than
Teenage of Insanity
Touch of Friendship
Wedding Wonders
Words From the Coach

Perpetual Calendars

365 Reasons to Eat Chocolate
Always Remember Who Loves Y
Best Friends
Coffee Breaks
The Dog Ate My Car Keys
Extraordinary Women
Foundations of Leadership
Generations
The Heart That Loves
The Honey Jar
I Think My Teacher Sleeps at Sch
I'm a Little Stressed
Keys to Success
Kid Stuff
Never Never Give Up
Older Than Dirt
Secrets of a Successful Mom
Shopoholic
Sweet Dreams
Teacher Zone
Tee Times
A Touch of Kindness
Apple a Day
Golf Forever
Quotes From Great Women
Teacher Are First Class